Two and one-half years in Hell on Earth

Reverend Willie L. Pounds, Author

TWO AND ONE-HALF years in Hell on Earth

A story of a family that struggles to overcome the horrific cruelties and inequalities of segregation, sharecropping, and plantation life while living in Arkansas and Louisiana!

Copyright © 2020 Willie L Pounds

No part of this book may be reproduced or transmitted in any form or by any means: graphic, electronic, or mechanical, including photocopying, recording, taping, or by any information storage retrieval system without permission, in writing, of the publisher or author.

Lowbar Publishing Company
905 S. Douglas Ave.
Nashville, Tennessee 37204
615-972-2842
Lowbarpublishingcompany@gmail.com
www.Lowbarbookstore.com
Author: Willie L. Pounds
Editor: Theophilus Odeh
Format Artist: Aalishaa
Graphic and Cover Design Artist: Norah S. Branch

Printed in the United States of America
ISBN: 978-1-7329202-5-5

For additional information or to contact the author for workshops or seminars, please email the author, willbs2004@yahoo.com or Lowbar Publishing Company.

Table of Contents

Part I: The creation and struggles of a family 1

    Dedication 2

    Introduction: 3

    My Father 7

    My Father's Marriages 10

Part 2: The overcoming of plantations' barriers 15

    Plantation Life 16

    A historical record of Abowitz Plantation 26

    The Hell Plantation 29

    Head of Household under duress 33

    Lunchtime entertainment 36

    Work or be beaten 38

The thrill of meeting mary lee 46

My New Life With Jesus 53

The Family Photo Gallery...61

PART 1

The creation and struggles of a family

Dedication

Dedicated To My Father and Mother

This book is dedicated to the late Zeb and Bessie Mae Coger Pounds. They labored hard and taught the family the importance of sacrificing their own lives to make a better future for future generations.

Introduction:

My Grandmother, Grandfather, and Mother Bessie Mae

Cubie Coger, my grandfather, was a Blackfoot and Cree Indian. He was born in 1874 in Alabama, and he married Mannie Jones, my grandmother, on January 14, 1909, at the age of twenty-five. Mammie was born in 1889 in Alabama, and she married at the age of twenty. To this union, three children were born: Bessie, Truedell, and

Forest. Bessie, my mother, was born on May 9, 1910, and died on April 28, 1948. She had two other siblings, who were born on the family land in Tuscaloosa, Alabama. Mammie died when she was thirty-one, and when Cubie, her husband, was forty-six. After the death of my grandmother, Mammie Jones Coger, Grandpa Cubie Coger decided to leave his hometown. With the help of his relatives, he packed up his children and moved to Arkansas on a plot of land just outside of Marianna, which he later purchased. His land in Alabama was to be purchased by a relative named Mrs. Clods Rutledge, who promised to send the money to Truedell Coger Lewis, Grandpa's second-oldest daughter. Aunt Truedell, my mother's sister, learned of Clods Ruthledge many years later after she had found her father and contacted her. She never knew if Mrs. Clods Ruthledge purchased the land.

My grandfather, Cubie Coger, had to deal with the death of his wife, coupled with the burden of having total responsibility for the kids. He never thought Mammie would ever leave him or die before him—it came as a surprise—leaving him with three children. Grandpa Coger could not overcome the death of Mammie, and he never accepted the total responsibility of the children: Bessie Mae, my mother, age nine, Truedell, my aunt, age seven, and Forest, age five. He could not imagine our grandmother leaving him or dying. Her unfortunate demise was a big shock to him. After relocating to Moore, Arkansas, Grandpa Coger fell in love with a young woman in Marianna named Ludie Ford. She did not have children of her own, and she was not willing to take care of his children. She desired to raise her own children and not another woman's children. Grandpa Coger had to decide between a life with her and a life without his children. It was a very difficult decision, so he asked Ludie to allow his children to live with her sister, his sister-in-law.

Grandpa was not aware that Ludie's sister did not want to take care of his children. Thus, his children were mistreated. Ludie's sister tied the children up each day to keep them out of her food and personal items.

Sometimes she tied them up for hours, and even for a day, without food or water. Some days, the kids would get loose to clean up and feed themselves before she returned home. The children were in constant conflict with her because she hated having them in her house, and Grandpa Coger never knew that she was abusing his children. One day, Aunt Truedell overheard Ludie's plans to send the three children away on trains, each one to a different location, on different days. The oldest, Bessie Mae, would be the first to go. The next day, Ludie intended to send the second oldest, Truedell, and the third day the last child, Forest. All three children were to be sent on separate trains until they all were gone.

The children were eleven, nine, and seven years of age, respectively, when Ludie took them to a nearby train station and sent them to different cities in different states. The children cried, but she sent each of them away at different times, on different trains, and in different directions. The family never learned of Forest's relocation, and he did not reunite with the family. Truedell relocated to West Memphis, and Bessie Mae, our mother, was found crying on a train headed southbound between Pine Bluff and Dermott, Arkansas, by a Lady named Mrs. Moriah Keller.

Mrs. Keller traveled from Dermott to Pine Bluff sometimes bi-monthly, visiting distant relatives. She said she saw a child crying and asked, "Little girl, where are you going? And why are you crying?" Bessie's reply was, "I don't know where I am going. I am looking for my daddy." Mrs. Keller then asked, "Where do you live?" And Bessie said, "I don't know." Mrs. Keller then asked, "What is your name and how old are you?" Bessie answered, "My name is Bessie Mae Coger, and I am eleven years old." Mrs. Keller, concerned for Bessie's safety, asked her questions because she was a very tall and beautiful young girl.

Mrs. Keller asked Bessie if she would come live with her, and she would try to help find her family. Excited, Bessie said, "Yes, ma'am!" So, Mrs. Keller took Bessie Mae home to live with her until they could locate her parents, but their search was inevitably unsuccessful. And after living with the Kellers a few years, Bessie became a member of Keller's family. Mr. and Mrs. Keller did not have children of their own. They did not change Bessie's last name for fear of stripping her hope of ever finding her family.

My Father

Zeb, my father, was the grandson of a slave named Walsh Pounds. His family was free to leave Canada in 1875 alone with the Griffins and many other relatives and friends. They traveled together south until they finally reached an area called Wilmot, Arkansas. After observing the area, they surmised no one claimed ownership of the land. The plot of land the Pounds settled on included a small lake about 1,000 feet in diameter, surrounded by Oak and Cyprus trees, which was good for building. The lake was a needed resource for food and water. So, they began to build houses and plant crops for their food and build shelters for the upcoming winter. Walsh later had a son, and he named him Wench. He had a second son named Winston Sterling Pounds Jr.

The two sons grew up and started dating girls. Wench met a girl named Florence Broughton in 1899. She became pregnant, and on June 27, 1900, she gave birth to twin boys: Zeb, my father, and Zeffie. Months after the babies were born, Zeffie had complications with breathing and later died. Florence' stepfather angrily warned her of having babies out of wedlock. He told her that if it happened again, she would have to leave. The following year, she had a daughter named Esther, and her stepfather put the three of them out of the home. It broke her mother's heart, and she tried to convince her husband to let them stay, but he said no.

My grandfather saw his daughter as a disgrace to the community. But Florence, my grandmother, prayed, and somehow the Lord worked it out. There was only one white family in the community at that time, and they agreed to take her and the three children to live with them, and they could use extra help with the house cleaning. Florence' son, Zeb, was unhappy living with white people. He wanted to live with his own father's family, but they didn't want him.

Zeb could not bear the hurt and rejection of his father and grandparents. There was a time when having children out of wedlock was a dishonor to the family and a sin before God. His grandfather became a Methodist preacher in the community. Winston embarrassed his family; therefore, they refused to accept the children he had out of wedlock. In other words, the Pounds family did not accept Zeb's mother nor his sister Esther. Florence loved Winston, and they kept their relationship. When Zeb was 11 years old, he ran away from home to explore life and make it on his own. After he had been gone for a few years, his father decided to marry his mother, Florence Broughton, and they brought their family together. Zeb was the oldest living of seven children.

The names of his siblings were Zeb, Esther, Edmond, Matthew, Henry, and Sterling Winston Jr. When Zeb was 17 years old, he finally came back home to the place where he was born so he could apologize to his mother for running away and worrying her all those years. Only to learn that he had missed her funeral by a few weeks. He was deeply hurt to learn that his mother was deceased, and he would never see her face again. It made him sad and angry. So, he left home this time and never tried to communicate with his immediate family or grandparents anymore.

While he was home, Zeb didn't communicate with his father. The bitterness his father held for him drove Zeb to leave again. This time, with no intention of ever returning. Zeb was a hurt man without the hope of ever having a mother in his life again. He had hoped to apologize to her for leaving home the way he did. But now, Zeb had to live the rest of his life without ever telling her how sorry he was for hurting her. As a young man, he never thought of being married, but after leaving his family this time, he desired to have a female companion. Zeb began to look for a wife.

My Father's Marriages

After leaving his parents, Zeb traveled to Trip-Junction, Arkansas, where he met and married his first wife. Over the next three years, they had three lovely children: two girls and one boy. The names of the children of his first wife are unknown to me. My father only mentioned he left them behind. They lived with his mother-in-law for approximately three years after they were married. Sitting around the fire at night, dad would tell us about his first wife and how his mother-in-law took all his money. People spread rumors that she used voodoo or magic to cast a spell on him to take all his money every week. His wife didn't seem to care about what others had to say. He tried to work things out with her, but she wanted to stay with her mother, so he finally left her and got divorced. Leaving the children behind, he traveled to Arkansas City at the age of twenty. And in 1920, he met and married a young lady named Rosie Brown, and she truly loved him, nicknaming Zeb, "ZB." He stayed with her for a year and a half before divorcing her. Unfortunately, Rosie Brown could not have children, and even though Zeb decided to move on, they remained friends for life.

He moved again to Dermott, Arkansas, not very far from his birthplace, but he never sought to reunite with his family back in Wilmot. While in Dermott, Arkansas, he met the Kellers and lived in their guesthouse in the back of their home. This was where Zeb, my father, met Bessie, my mother. They met at the home of Mr. and Mrs. Moriah Keller. Mr. Keller and Zeb worked together at a chicken barn in the city, where they killed and plucked chickens' feathers. My mother, Bessie, cleaned the main house daily. The Kellers deemed the cleaning of their home and the guesthouse to be enough for her living expenses.

Since Mrs. Keller brought Bessie home, over the previous two years, to live with them, she was treated as a member of the family. With very little education, she learned how to work hard for her living, and during that time, Bessie and Zeb got together. He was her senior by ten years. They got in a secret relationship for a few months, which led to her getting pregnant with their first child. When the Kellers learned that Bessie was pregnant and Zeb was the father, it made them very unhappy. They demanded that he marry her as soon as the baby was born or face a shotgun. After the baby arrived in 1923, they got married. That same year, she turned thirteen, and their daughter was the largest child they would have. Dad said that she weighed 16 and ¼ pounds.

After a year passed, my father and my mother moved away from the Kellers' home to make it on their own. Zeb was skilled in many things, such as farming, building, automotive mechanics, and cleaning chickens. They later moved to a place called Gains Landing. Gains Landing was a part of Turner Neal Plantation just northeast of Arkansas City on the levee. They made their home there. Soon, Bessie had her firstborn son, Eugene, and the following year, twins. Due to the lack of medical knowledge in those times, they died shortly after birth. There was a horse corral on the plantation, not very far from the house where dad kept the mules. One afternoon when Eugene was playing, he crawled under the fence, and one of the mules stepped on him, which caused him to suffer from horrible injuries. Dad took Eugene to McGehee, Arkansas, to a medical doctor, but he didn't seem to get better. At the same time, my mother was recovering after giving birth to stillborn twins. She mourned their death. My father fished to take his mind away from what was going on around him. During this time, my mother was praying and wondering what had happened to her father, sister, and brother.

Mother said that she didn't know that while she was praying, God had already answered her prayer. After eight long years, she had a reunion with her sister. Truedell traveled from Little Rock, Arkansas, to Der-Mott, Arkansas, where she learned from the Kellers that Bessie, my mother, had married and had a baby. In 1924, Zeb and Bessie moved away from Der-Mott to Arkansas City, Arkansas, on the levee. Aunt Truedell traveled by train, cars, wagons, and foot, stopping for directions along the way, seeking to reunite with her sister. And as she got closer to the house, she saw a lady in a chair but did not know that it was her sister, my mother, sitting on the porch. As Truedell walked along the dirt road, and the closer she got to the house, the more my mother was unrecognizable to her. She introduced herself after stepping upon the porch. They talked for a few minutes, and then Truedell and my mother recognized each other. Crying and hugging, they held on to each other for what seemed like an hour.

As they cried, they shared small parts of their story. After their discussion, Bessie, my mother, learned that her sister Truedell had traveled north to West Memphis, Arkansas. Ludie, their stepmother, had sent her to West Memphis, Arkansas, by train. A nice family received her in their home for a few years, but later they sent her to North Little Rock.

While in North Little Rock, she met a young man named Bud Watson. Soon after meeting him, they got married. In those days, Bud worked as a porter on the trains. It was a good job for blacks. Later that afternoon, when my father, Zeb, got back home from fishing, he saw his sister-in-law, Truedell, for the first time. He was happy and surprised. He had heard so much about her. Aunt Truedell had no idea what she would find when she located her sister. She could not imagine my mother, Bessie, having given birth to so many children.

After staying with us for many days, Aunt Truedell went back to North Little Rock, Arkansas. She made many weekend trips to visit her sister and our family until the levee broke. For years, dad would sit around the fire and tell the family about Arkansas City. Before the flood, he said that it was a bi-culture city and had two theaters within the city. Levees surrounded Arkansas City to prevent flooding when the river rose during high tide. Catastrophic flooding occurred in 1927 in Arkansas City, destroying almost everything in its path. The Mississippi River swelled so high that it broke the levee, flooding the city with over 30 feet of mud, sand, and water. The flood killed livestock, people, and destroyed most of the businesses. The Mississippi Riverboat docking stationed across the levee, by the Red Star grocery store was washed away. Before the flood, Arkansas City was very prosperous with the ports as its main industry. Steamboats traversed up and down the river making two or three stops weekly.

People from different cities, countries, and nationalities no longer visited Arkansas City. The devastating 1927 flood all but wiped Arkansas City off the map. However, the city slowly recovered years later after the flood. By that time, there were two dry goods stores, one bank, three nightclubs, two liquor stores, two grocery stores, Chum and Jack Chinaman stores, Mr. Eddie Robertson restaurant, Mr. Calvin Price restaurant/club, and Miss Mattie's restaurant/club, one post office, two gas stations, two ice cream parlors, Red Star Grocery, one closing store, and one bait shop. After the great flood, the river completely changed to a murky brown color. The riverboats could no longer come close to the city ending its trade with the city.

The Abowitz Plantation's cowboys were Mr. Percy and Mr. Bunch Ringo. They rode Pinto Horses. Mr. Bunch Ringo had a daughter named Kathrine. She was very flashy. She wore Daisey dukes' short pants years before the trend. She drove Ford cars with green-white and red-white color options. She would buy a new car every two years.

In Arkansas City, her father was one of the cowboys that herded the cattle from across the levee to the stockyard and barn on the north side of the town. It became a great expansion to the Abowitz Plantation. They herded the cows over the levee to the stockyard once a year. Trains from the city of McGhee located on the side of the levee would back into the docks in the south of the town. The cowboys wrangled the cows through the town to load them on the train. Dad could not read very well, but he always spoke verbal history by the fire, keeping us informed of our past. Somehow, he learned from a rumor, in the year 1929 back in Wilmot, Arkansas, that his father's brother, Winston Sterling Jr. (Poundy), was caught two years earlier in a white man's home having sex with his wife and was later found hanging by his neck from a tree in the community. They also found his bicycle nearby, but they never did find out who murdered him.

Later, my father Zeb learned that his father, Winston, the senior, had died in 1935, but he never received any information from the family concerning the funeral arrangement. mom and dad continued to have children. In 1940, my mother gave birth to a baby girl and named her Truedell after her sister. In 1941, my mother, Bessie, had a miscarriage of twins. In 1942, my brother was born, and daddy named him Zeb Jr. and nicknamed him Bo. In 1943, another set of twins was stillborn, and in 1944, I was born, and my sister Willie B. asked my mother if she could give me her name. Mother said, "Yes," and she named me Willie Lee Pounds.

As we became young boys, Mr. Turner Neal, who owned a plantation next to the Abowitz Plantation, saw my brother Bo and me. He asked our daddy if he could buy the two of us. Our father and our mother said no!! He said that "we were very good-looking boys," and he wanted to do great things with us, but dad said that he could not see himself giving us up. In 1946, mom gave birth to a baby girl. The midwife said the baby was having health issues upon delivery. The little girl died weeks later. That same year, the family moved to the Abowitz Plantation, located on Highway 4, which was approximately four miles west of Arkansas City, Arkansas.

PART 2

The overcoming of plantations' barriers

Plantation Life

The Abowitz Plantation was owned by Jews. They were different from other plantations' owners. Dad said that he had never seen the Jews beat or rape any of the workers; they were nice to all of them. They made sure that everyone worked in harmony. The Abowitz only had one white man over the plantation store, yet all the blacks, whites, and Mexicans got along well while living on the plantation working together. Even the children had fun playing together on the farm. There was a large bayou that divided the Kennedy Farm from the Abowitz Plantations; children fished and swam together in the stream. One day, dad took Bo and me to the plantation store. It was a small shotgun building located next to the main homestead. It was my first time being in the store, and it was exciting being in the store surrounded by barrels of candy. While dad was shopping, Bo and I filled our pockets with free candy, or at least we thought the candy was free.

The storekeeper caught us red-handed and told our dad. We had to give all the candy back to the clerk, and we still got the worse whipping for picking up things that were not ours. We learned the hard way not to take things that did not belong to us. In the spring of 1947, another brother was born. Now, Aunt Truedell always came down from North Little Rock to be with our mother during the delivery of her new babies. We always eagerly awaited her arrival because she brought clothes for everybody, some old and some new. As young children, we didn't understand that Aunt Truedell was hurting over the loss of her first husband, Uncle Bud. She still came down to spend time with our mother and the family despite her grief.

On this occasion, Aunt Truedell surprised our mother when she asked if she could name the new baby, and our mother gladly granted her permission. In April 1947, our mother gave birth to a baby boy, and Auntie named him Arthur Antonio Miller Pounds. Some people from our mother's church family were not in agreement with the baby's name. Since she loved the church so much and attended every time she was not busy, they tried to encourage my mother to choose a Christian name from the Bible. The community's women always praised my mother, Bessie, for her commitment to the church, God, and her family. On Sunday mornings, mom always had a line of children walking down Highway 4 to Zion Hill Missionary Baptist Church. It was located just down the road on the right, across from a ditch on a small hill.

Washington's and Fuqua's families didn't attend church very often, but they always praised our mother for the way she cleaned and dressed her children. She slicked our hair down with hog lard. Mother was the talk of the community because she made sure that her children were clean and pretty. Dad had favor with the Abowitz Plantation's owner. Therefore, he was permitted to fish for extra food and money for the family in the Mississippi River across the levee and Boggy Bayou. He did very well during the winter months when the work was slow, while the other workers had to keep the livestock fed. In the late forties and early fifties, Mr. Sam Abowitz purchased Ford tractors to do the work on the farm. They were very small tractors with two-bladed braking plows and all one roe equipment.

When the weather was warmer, the workers were responsible for getting the equipment ready for a spring groundbreaking. Dad was one of the men who were responsible for that task. When breaking time came, the ground was black and very hard. They called it "buckshot" because it was difficult to prepare for planting cotton and corn. Cattle, horses, and sheep roamed near Boggy Bayou. Most of the cattle were moved across the levee from Arkansas City and traveled west to the stockyard, where they were sold.

The Abowitz Plantation was the largest in the city. Sam Abowitz came to Arkansas City from Brooklyn, New York, in 1918 as a merchant and later became a Levee Contractor and helped build the Mississippi River levees. He later purchased 1,200 acres that became the Boggy Bayou Plantation. He cleared the land with cross-cut saws and a team of mules. Besides the barns and the big house, there were ten other tenant houses on the farm.

As I would sit and listen to my older siblings, I learned that mom and dad were always concerned about raising and nurturing their children right. They didn't have much education back in those days, but what they had was known as wit, grit, and intuition. Mother and Father had good ole' common sense as they taught each of their children the responsibilities and what it took to raise a family. They allowed the oldest siblings to name the younger siblings and allowed them to care for them. Mother knew that this would help teach the oldest girls how to be good mothers to their own children someday. So, after twenty-five years of marriage and nineteen children—nine died, and only ten lived—the family moved off the Abowitz Plantation to the Prude Farm, just two miles west of Arkansas City, on Highway 4. It was adjacent to the Abowitz Plantation.

The greatest thing about the move was that mom was closer to Zion Hill Missionary Baptist Church and her women friends. We were next door to Mr. Henry Fuqua's family and Washington's house. The Washingtons were the only family in the area that could come close to matching our family since they had ten children. A month before her 39th birthday, on April 28, 1948, at the age of 38, our loving mother cooked her last big supper for the family. She was washing the family's laundry in the washtub with a scrubbing board on the west side of the house when she fell out with a sunstroke, according to Doctor Coleman. Doctor Coleman was the only doctor in town that people of color could consult. He looked like a white man only because his daddy was white. Dr. Coleman was in his mid-fifties. He was tall with gray hair. He came to our house to announce the ugly news of our mother's death. He said that our mother had a massive stroke. That day, our mother, Bessie, left her family—our dad and ten of us—behind and went to be with Jesus, and we didn't know how to follow her.

Daddy was never concerned about the Church and God; he thought that it was just another way of enslaving the minds of Black people. Mother was the only hope in our family for any of the children to get to know Jesus Christ as our Lord and Savior. After she died, it was very difficult for our father. He never thought mom would die or leave us like that. The family was blessed to have our older sisters to take care of the younger siblings, but within the next year after Mother Bessie died, our family went through many storms. Our oldest sister, Bestell, had married Mr. Robert Patterson before mom died. He was a short, thin, dark man with a head full of long hair all down his back. Mr. Patterson had an amputated right leg made from wood. They had a little girl, two-years of age, named Mary Lee Patterson. They lived in a shack in Arkansas City with no running water, no electricity, and a wood stove with a dirt floor

And soon after Mother passed, our sister, Mary Lee Pounds, got pregnant with a little girl by a man from Lake Village, Arkansas, named Felton. She moved to North Little Rock, Arkansas, to live near our Aunt Truedell. Dad didn't have much to do with Aunt Truedell after the death of our mother. By 1949, our father tried to get a woman's support in the home, but with little success. So, Auntie came down from North Little Rock in 1949 and asked dad if she could have my brother Arthur to keep and raise. Father said yes, and she took him back to North Little Rock, Arkansas, to stay with her. Dad moved back to the Abowitz Plantation, where he met and fell in love with a housekeeping woman, Miss Estell. She was only twenty-one years old, and she was his fourth wife. Mrs. Estell Hedgeman gave birth to a boy in 1951 and named him E-Zell. In 1952, she gave birth to a little girl and named her Thelma. She only lived about three or four weeks before she died of complications. That same year, my sister Willie B. enrolled my brother Bo and me in J.B. Payne School in Arkansas City. I was almost seven years old. The city boys didn't like us, country boys, too well, especially the Ward brothers.

They were so mean. They fought us every day on the playground and even before we got on the school bus. They hated the name Pounds. We would cry the whole four miles to the plantation. When Willie B. would meet us at the bus stop, she would ask us why we were crying, and we would tell her everything that had happened. Then, she would whip us for letting the boys beat us. She would also ask us to report the incident to the schoolteacher. That same year around Easter, daddy decided to take his new wife and load up all his children on his flatbed A-model Ford and travel from Arkansas City through the back gate to the Mississippi River to watch the riverboats. The ferry carried cars across the river to De-Witt, Arkansas, where our cousin, Mrs. Felida, lived. We didn't cross the river. We ate and played, then loaded-up and traveled back to Arkansas City.

Months later, my father moved from the Abowitz Plantation to the Turner Neal Plantation near Bayou-Mason, Arkansas. When we lived there, I was about seven years old. Dad, Bo, and I worked together with the mules preparing the field for planting cotton. The Charlestons lived on the plantation, and they had a large family of four boys and two girls. Of course, other families were working on the land as well. Dad taught Bo and me how to catch and harness the mules. Easy to work with, it seemed as if the mules knew what to do without us. So, they would open their mouths for the beats and lower their head down for us to put the bridle on them.

The horses' names were Diamond, the red one, and Shine, the gray one. We always had fun working with the horses. One day, dad sent Bo and me to the house just before lunch with a note to take to the store to pick up some food. But when we got to the store and gave the note to the storekeeper, he said, "Tell your dad that he cannot have any food until he talks with Mr. Turner Neal." When dad got home from the field, we told him what the storekeeper said. Dad got mad and went back to the store to confront the keeper. They began to exchange words, and dad said that he was going over the hill to talk with Mr. Turner Neal. The storekeeper didn't take his words kindly and got angry with dad and threw a coke bottle at him. The bottle missed my father and struck the door beside him, and the shattered pieces of glass cut his hand.

When dad saw the blood, he turned and said to the storekeeper, "You cut my hand?" The storekeeper said, "I intended to knock you out, Nigger." Dad, raging mad, walked over to the counter, and jumped up and grabbed the storekeeper by his collar. He pulled the storekeeper down on the countertop with his right hand, and with his bloody left fist, he beat the keeper's face until he knocked him out. The storekeeper's wife came out and stopped the fight by screaming, "You killed my husband!" Dad went to Mr. Turner Neal's home after the confrontation. He told Mr. Neal everything that happened and how he thought he killed a white man. Mr. Turner Neal told him to go back home and that he was going to take care of the matter. Consequently, Mr. Turner Neal fired the white storekeeper. Mr. Neal then asked dad to come back to the store for his groceries, and dad didn't have any more problems from that incident.

After the crops were all planted within the coming months, dad decided to pack up and move away from Arkansas. In 1953, dad talked to Mr. Richard Henry Hedgeman about giving his daughter Geraldine to marry Mr. Hedgeman's son, Joe Hedgeman, who lived in Green Bayou Ridge, Louisiana. They discussed it all night, and by morning, Mr. Hedgeman decided to give his blessing to the marriage.

Dad went to Willie B.'s house to tell her that he changed his mind about letting her keep me because I was living with both my sister Willie B. and dad sometimes. Since my sister Geraldine was living in Louisiana, dad decided to move to Del-hi, Louisiana. We came to her house to tell her that he was taking me with him to meet with Mrs. Estell's family, not knowing that she had a younger sister.

In 1955, my brother E-Zell was four. My sister Thelma died, and Willie B. was the baby. Shortly after we moved, Estell told the family about her sister named Geneva Tate, and that she had been married but left her husband and returned home. Everyone in town said that she was brown-skinned with short brown hair and built like a coke bottle, so she left her husband back in Camden, Arkansas. Geneva and her baby girl came to live with her sister Estell, and my father. After we moved to Del-hi, my sister Geraldine, who was married to Joe Hedgeman, had their second child, Adeline. Their first child, Joe Jr., died shortly after his birth. They traveled to dad's house and asked if they could take me to live with them for a little while. They lived about 12 miles northeast of Epps, Louisiana, and approximately 16 miles from Lake Providence, Louisiana.

While I lived with them, I would babysit in the car while they went dancing on Lakefront Street in Lake Providence, Louisiana, on Saturday nights. Now in Lake Providence, they would say that the men that got off the boats were sharply dressed. They had big hats, baggie pants with long chains, and they would party all night long. It didn't matter how long my sister and her husband stayed out on Saturday nights. They would rest on Sunday. One Monday morning, they tried hard to enroll me in school, but they were not successful because it was very difficult to get me back and forth to school due to the lack of fare. I was still in the second grade at age 11, and I didn't seem to fit anywhere anymore.

I really wanted to go back to Arkansas City to live with Willie B., but I had no voice in the matter, even the idea seemed impossible. As soon as my sister Geraldine got me to settle down, I was okay. My greatest joy was sitting with my baby niece named Adeline, with whom I had lots of fun caring for her. I bought my niece a little silver rocking chair, and it was difficult to keep her out of it. It was my job to babysit her every day, especially Saturday nights, while my sister and her husband, Joe, danced the night away. It was also my job every day to watch her while they were away at work. My brother-in-law had a sister named Thelma; we called her Tudor. She and her husband Melvin also lived in Green Bayou Ridge in the rural countryside just down the road from us, and she was crazy. She would pick on me all the time. I figured it was because she had no children of her own at the time. She would catch me and pull my pants down and tell everybody to look at my little wee-wee, short for penis. My sister Geraldine never stopped her from messing with me.

The word got out that Melvin was courting around with our sister, Truedell, and her best friend, Honey. She was very light-complexioned with short hair, and everyone called her "red cow." No one told Thelma about the relationship that went on for months. As I recall, my sister's husband, Joe, had a brother named R.L. He and I were the same age, and we played together. Truedell and Honey had a certain place where they would eat dirt from the ground. R.L. and I found out the spot where they ate dirt, and if they got mad with us about anything, we told them that we were going to pee on their dirt. They wanted to beat us, but Geraldine would not allow them to touch the two of us. We never did pee on their dirt.

I remember one day during the summer months when I was babysitting Adeline while my sister and her husband, Joe, were away, and the baby was asleep, R.L. and I played outside on a stack of old lumber. I stepped on a rusty nail, and it went completely through my right foot. We were young boys and didn't know how to treat it or what to do; it hurt badly. I only knew to step on the board and lift my foot off the nail. The pain became more intense. It wasn't long before my sister came home, and I was crying, and the baby was also crying. I didn't understand why my head was hurting so badly; it felt like it would burst at any time. Geraldine said that I almost had lockjaw from the rusty nail. She wrapped a piece of salted pork fat meat around my foot and poured kerosene on it, my foot hurt even more for days and nights.

She said the salt pork fat was supposed to draw out the infection and keep the swelling down. I didn't get any sleep at all for days. Once my foot began to heal and feel better, they took me to the cotton field to help with the baby and pick a little cotton. I liked living with my sister and playing with R.L. Hedgeman. The Hedgeman loved eating black bears and goats. They ate little or no pork. Every holiday, we ate bear and goat meats. They prepared the meat by digging a hole in the ground. They would build a fire in the hole for cooking the meat over the opened flames.

At a young age, Geraldine, my sister, taught me how to cook. During the holidays, she would teach me how to bake cakes and pies. She said that every boy needed to know how to cook because someday, he might need to do it for himself. R.L. had a sister named Dorothy. I always thought she liked me, and I didn't understand why. I guess it was a "girl" thing. We would play with the other children, having fun, gathering wood, and keeping the fire going while waiting for the food to be cooked and served.

Meanwhile, back in Del-hi, Louisiana, something went very wrong at my father's house between him and his wife, Mrs. Estell. Our sister, Jessie, five-feet tall, and her alcoholic husband, Walter Lee Davis, who stood about six feet eight inches tall, were both mean and dangerous. When they moved to Del-hi, Louisiana, from Dermott, Arkansas, Walter became so hooked on alcohol until he would burn Rubbing alcohol and drink it. They wanted to move in with my father. My father's wife, Estell, insisted on moving out of the house if they moved in. She warned dad that if he allowed them to move in, she would leave, and he would never see his children again.

E-Zell was 4, and Willie D. was just a small baby. She also had two other young children when she married my father, Zeb. The children were Dorothy and a boy named Johnny. So, she moved and left the state of Louisiana, or so we thought. She told no one where she was going. Dad said that she made him very sad, lonely, and hurt by leaving him. In the meantime, my older brother, Bo, had a crush on a girl named Geneva and tried to talk to her, but she treated him like a little boy. Later, dad started talking to teenage girls, and before we knew it, dad brought Geneva to live with him. And In 1956, we had a new stepmom, only nineteen years old. My father would later say that he was trying to find another woman like my mother, Bessie Mae. But no woman could ever fill that void, not even Geneva!

A historical record of Abowitz Plantation

The Abowitz family sold the farm to Judge J.F. Wallace in 1993. Later that year, Judge Wallace died and left the farm to a charitable trust. In 1994, the trustees applied to enroll the farm, the Wetland Reserve Program, in the winter of 1996 – 1997. The Boggy Bayou "Farm" is being nominated to the Arkansas Register of Historic Places under Criterion C for its depiction of a Depression-era tenant farmstead. The plantation is not considered for inclusion in the National Register of Historic Places because of the asphalt plate siding on the main tenant house. The trustees of the farm, however, are considering removing the artificial siding and restoring the original cypress weatherboard siding. If this restoration occurs, the property would then be eligible for the National Registry.

Counterclockwise from Center: Main Barn, Store/One-Room Shack, Main Horse Barn, 2 Work Barns, Equipment Work Barn, Tractor Barn, and Four-Room Shack

Recreation of Abowitz Plantation

The Hell Plantation

Between the years of 1956 and 1959, in a small-town named Don-nell, Louisiana, our family moved from the Hedgeman and Whitehead's farm in Del-hi, Louisiana, to Epps, Louisiana. Dad heard that blacks were treated fairly on Hell's sharecropper farm and could go and come as they pleased. Our family was taught by our father how to obey men who had authority or charge over us, even when they were the enemies of the family. In these two and a half years, I would experience hatred and witness the sexual abuse of my sister and stepmother by our overseers. My stepmother was raped when she was two months pregnant with her second child. Dad would later tell the family that he had no real hope of ever making a living on the Hell Plantation.

Not long after dad married, we moved to the Hell Farm. The Hell Farm operated just like a plantation located just outside of Don-nell, Louisiana. My father said that the Hells wanted every child that was healthy and able to work to be living on the plantation. Therefore, dad picked me up from Geraldine's house and took me to live with him in Don-nell, Louisiana. I was eleven years old at the time when I reunited with my brother, Zeb Jr., nicknamed Bo, who was thirteen at that time. After a few days, our family went to meet Hell's family. They had four brothers: Louis was the oldest, and Elsie was blind. Conley thought he was a heartbreaker, and Bill was the youngest. The Hells had a host of other relatives. Three of the brothers had sons and daughters.

They let the black and white kids work together. The kids also played together sometimes on the plantation with the other families that were on the farm. One of my many jobs was to prepare the nightly bath water for Mr. Elsie's household. The white boys played a game among themselves called "grab-ass." They would not let me play with them, and they said that only the white kids could play this game, and niggers couldn't play it. They would put their penises in each other's mouth and stick it in each other's rectum. I was not sure if the act was okay or not. The only thing that I knew was that they had lots of fun, or at least it seemed like they had. Every night, the boys would play "grab ass" while taking their baths. I could only look on. I always had a big mess to clean up before going to my house.

My brother Bo also had evening jobs, which always included keeping the fire burning in the smokehouse and running errands. I recall that he was out in the smokehouse one evening, which was located about twenty feet from the back door of Mr. Elsie's house, cooling the fire by putting sawdust on it. He told me that Craig's youngest sister, Sandra, who was only eleven years of age, and flirtatious, always tried to catch him in the smokehouse and kiss him. He said that he was afraid for his life because he just knew that the Hells would hang him. At that time in my life, I didn't understand why she wanted to kiss him in the first place, or why they would kill him for that. One night, Mr. Elsie sent Bo to the store in his new black 1956 Ford pickup truck. Craig and I jumped in the truck with Bo, so we could have something to do. We made it to the store in Don-nell, Louisiana, and on our way back home, Craig and I played in the front seat. We were having so much fun that we did not realize we had hit Bo, causing him to lose control. Thus, he wrecked the new truck. I busted my lip and broke my front tooth on the dashboard. We had to walk about a mile back to the house. I was the only one bleeding and crying and was in extreme pain for my tooth had cut through my top lip.

That night, we walked into Mr. Elsie's house with blood all over my clothes. Mrs. Maxine explained what she saw to her husband, and he became angry and put us out of his house that night. But the next morning, Bo and Craig had to answer for wrecking Mr. Elsie's new black Ford truck. Injured, I was unable to report for work, but he beat Bo and Craig for wrecking his truck. The Hells were evil people; they hated everybody, including themselves.

I was in Mr. Elsie's house one day, not knowing that the adults were home, and his brother Conley, the "playboy," was kissing Linda Faye, his 16-year-old niece, Mr. Elsie's oldest daughter. When I saw it, I turned and walked back out, hoping that he did not see me. I also remember walking in the house one day at lunchtime when Mrs. Maxine, Mr. Elsie's wife, was serving Mr. Elsie his food, and Conley was in the house with them rubbing and kissing Faye.

I thought to myself that the whole family had no morals or respect for each other. They treated each other the same way they treated the workers and black families on the plantation. They treated themselves as if they were only property.

My oldest sister, Bestell, and her husband, Jacey, Mrs. Eva, and her husband, Elmo, lived down the road behind Mr. Elsie's house. Our house was across the cow pasture from his home. The pasture ran behind the other houses and down into the field. The Hells worked approximately 300 acres of land, and they had approximately 100 herds of cows and four horses. They raised cotton, corn, Irish potatoes, sweet potatoes, and hay. Everyone on the farm had a job. And because the Hells had favor with all the local law enforcement (at least it seemed that way), it was hard for anyone to get away within a twenty-five miles radius from Don-nell, Louisiana, whether it was south to Del-HI, Louisiana, or north to Oak Grove, Louisiana.

If anyone wanted to leave after they moved on the plantation, they weren't able to leave without some retribution. Don-nell, Louisiana, was two miles from the plantation. The workers were not allowed to leave the plantation without permission. At that time, I guess you can say that we had not thought of leaving because everyone was afraid of losing their life, or maybe we were trying to stay alive in peace.

Head of Household under duress

Our dad was trying to be a good husband. So, he assigned each family member their responsibilities. He assigned Geneva, his wife, to be the family new water person while we worked in the field. She didn't have it easy. She was often attacked by blue racer-snakes. After discovering that she was pregnant, she didn't have to do the housework or fieldwork. Dad assigned all the work to the children. I remember one day, while our family was picking cotton in the field, dad sent Geneva to bring us some water. After she had been gone for some time, dad sent me to help her because he didn't want her to overwork.

As I walked down the road, near the tractor shed, on the right side of the road, directly across from the barn, I could hear men talking while holding Geneva down and having sex with her. I saw the two young white men pressing down on her, and she was crying: "No! No! No! Don't do this to me. I am going to have a baby!" But she didn't scream! I saw the whole thing, but I could not tell dad what I saw. I didn't want him to lose his life. They would have killed my father if he had tried to defend the honor of Geneva. Panicking, I had to think twice about what I would tell dad if he asked me about Geneva. Thank goodness, he didn't ask because Geneva came home shortly behind me.

She pretended like nothing ever happened, and dad never knew she was raped. Geneva never knew that I saw the whole thing. In 1957, she gave birth to a healthy little girl and named her Shirley. That same year, the Hells bought a one-row tiller and cotton picker. After harvest, they purchased a 60 John Deere diesel tractor with a small gasoline engine to start it. Mr. Elsie said he got it for Bo, and no one else could drive it except him. One day, as we were preparing a field to plant, before lunch, the breaking plow cut into a bee nest. The bees came after Bo and me. They continued to sting us until Bo stopped the tractor, and we jumped between the tires onto the ground. We stayed there until they stopped swarming. Our bodies were swollen. Once we finished plowing the field, it was dark. As we were coming back across a muddy area in the woods, where there were deep tracks, the tractor slipped into one of the deep tracks and got stuck.

We had to walk about two miles to our house that night. The next day, Mr. Elsie kicked the ground, cursed, and spat. He beat us before going down to pull the tractor out of the mud, saying, "Don't you ever get my tractor stuck like this again." Of course, Bo and I promised that we would be careful next time. As summer ended, all the white children prepared themselves for school. While we watched white children get ready to go to school, Bo and I asked if we could attend school. We used the opportunity to ask if we could attend Pioneer Elementary School. Mr. Elsie said we could attend school. However, we were only able to attend for two weeks. He pulled us out of school during fall and winter. He told us that we had to work and help feed the family.

It seemed strange that every time school started, we had to work harder than ever. We had to wrangle the cows and give them medication for pink eye and rotten hoof. We did this every year at the beginning of the fall and early winter. At first, it was a long and boring job because black kids were left on the plantation. Every morning, we fed and milked the cows in the barn. Being young people, we couldn't wait for springtime. We wanted to go outside and play with all the other kids, even though we would have to work very hard when spring and summer came. It didn't matter what happened on the farm. The young kids just wanted to get outside and play together. We worked hard every day, breaking ground for planting cotton, corn, and the garden until it was time to start cutting and baling hay again.

Lunchtime entertainment

Every day, the Hells had new schemes for entertainment. Whoever was the overseer of the field that day, after lunch, they would tell the white boys to beat-up the black boys. These attacks would happen like clockwork every day in the field during the summer after lunch. My brother fought for me each day. I could not fight well enough to defend myself; so, he took care of me. Dad called me "skin" because I was very thin and frail. The other kids were bigger than I. He always told Bo and me to stick together because we were all that we had. Dad always told me that I would never amount to anything because I was too frail to tote my own food. Bo and I would run holding hands. When the white boys got close to us, Bo would tell me to keep running. He would turn around and fight the boys one at a time until he knocked both down. Then, he would catch back up to me.

After he whipped the boys chasing us, we would sit down under a shade- tree until it was time to return to work. The white boys weren't as lucky as we were. Sometimes, they were beaten up badly by my brother. The parents of the white boys would get very angry with them and say to them, "How can you rule over niggers if you can't beat them down?" Their parents would kick their butts for letting a black child whip them. Another devilish entertainment in the afternoon was wife swapping. It was my belief that their wives knew what to expect after they drove Mr. Elsie to the field in the afternoon. Whichever wife would bring Mr. Elsie to the field that day, they would park far away under a shade tree, and he would get to have sex with one of his brother's wives.

As one of the black boys, we were told not to let anyone catch us, and if we got caught, it would mean big trouble for everyone. The only thing I liked about the hayfield was all the good food they served. Bo baled the hay while the rest helped load the trucks that were delivered back to the plantation each evening. The Hells would cut and bale the hay, based on percentages. Every night, we would take a big truckload of hay back to the plantation and unload it the next morning, while the dew was still settling on the cut hay. In the morning, when we arrived back at the hayfield, all we had left to do was service the equipment and go back to work in the fields.

I could not wait for lunchtime, because I knew that everyone would not be able to eat all their food. However, I hated that every day the white men wanted to have their amusement with the black boys by making the white boys fight the black boys until blacks were beaten down or until the whites boys were beaten down and too tired to fight any more. Consequently, at our houses, the white boys did not fight us. The Hells would buy food for everyone, including the plantation workers.

On each plantation worker's porch sat a box with bean, flour, macaroni, lard, rice, tomato paste, cornmeal, and salt meat. They would do the same thing when buying clothing; they would buy one size fit all. We could not decide for ourselves; we were told when to go and when to come. The Hells owned night clubs, and when it rained, and we couldn't work outside, they would take different workers and drop them off at their clubs to clean them up.

Work or be beaten

During harvesting, some kids were playing, throwing broken potatoes at one another while working in the potato patch. The Hells always had someone watching the kids at the other end of the field. And if you were caught playing, the Hells would come down through the field and whip everyone that was playing. Mr. Elsie, the blind brother, did most of the whipping. He could not see, and he would hit you everywhere, including your face and head. He took no responsibility for his action because he was blind, and he was always led by one of the other brothers. This day, it happened to be Conley Hell, the heartbreaker, that led him through the field, whipping every boy he got his hands on. When he called me, I was working next to my dad. I told him that if I needed a whipping, my dad would whip me because I was working next to him.

Conley Hell grabbed my arm and held me so Mr. Elsie could whip me. Later, I ask my dad why he allowed Mr. Elsie to whip me. He never said anything. The Hells always had something going on. Every weekend, they drank and partied. If the parties were on the plantation, which most of the time they were, they would use the young black boys to drive them down the plantation road. They would tell the driver which Negro's house to stop at, and one of them would get out of the truck, go into the house with a pistol and run the man out of the house. Sometimes, they would shoot a few rounds in the air, then go back to the house and rape the woman of the house. One Saturday night, one of the Hells ran my brother-in-law Jayce out of his house so that he could have sex with his wife. Jayce told my dad that it was a night that he would never forget. He had to stay low and crawl across the pasture to another house. He told my father that he could feel the heat from the bullets over his head. Jayce was a tall, dark slim man in stature

I am not sure if Jayce knew that when he was forced out of his house, one of the Hells would have sex with his wife.

Also, there were a man and a woman who lived on the plantation. Mr. Elmo and Mrs. Eva were a black family with no children of their own. She kept her little niece, whose name was Eva Jane. Their family lived below Bestell and Jayce. Our family had lived on the Hell Plantation roughly a year and a half before Mrs. Eva got pregnant and later had a little blonde headed, blue-eyed baby girl. She and Mr. Elmo were told to marry after she became pregnant. Mr. Elmo, her husband, knew that the child wasn't his because Eva worked for Mrs. Maxine, Mr. Elsie's wife, in the big house. Mr. Elsie had sex with Eva at his pleasure because Mrs. Maxine, Mr. Elsie's wife, never stayed at home. No one knew that she was pregnant. She was tall, brown-skinned, and large with short black hair. After her little blue-eyed baby girl was born, rumor had it that her husband, Elmo, just walked out into the field one day, and he was never seen anymore. Dad said that Mr. Elmo probably killed himself.

The same year, dad sent our sister Truedell away because she was continually sexually abused by the Hells' men. At that time, she was sixteen years of age. There was a black family named Anderson, who had a son named William. They lived on another small farm on the backside of the Hell Plantation. Before dad sent Truedell away, their son had seen our sister Truedell. He started slipping through the woods to see her every chance he got. Eventually, the Hells caught him on their plantation, and they made him work, chopping cotton all day without food or water. At the end of the workday, they whipped him and sent him back home through the woods. They told William that if they caught him on their property again, they would kill him. Later, dad allowed William and Truedell to get married, and they moved to William's father's farm. Later, Truedell visited with Geraldine, where she met Honey "Red Cow" and became close friends.

The Hells never forgave my father for allowing my sister Truedell to leave the plantation. Dad had to take a kicking and a beating from the Hells for letting her leave the plantation. As I reminisced on those days, it was rough because every black person on the plantation was called "Nigger," and everyone was treated as if they were animals. While living on the plantation, when the work was slow, the workers had to clean the Hells' nightclubs. These were times that they did not curse or kick us in our rear ends. They didn't even beat us with a cattle rope. When Hell's family had cookouts on Saturdays, during the summer months, the white kids had lots of fun playing together without the interference of their white parents. For their entertainment, they had wild gray cows called Brangus with humps on their backs. They were very dangerous. They would make some of the black men go in the corral and catch them. Sometimes, the men would be badly injured, and nothing was ever said about it.

In those times, Bo and I were inseparable because dad made us swear never to let anyone come between us or cause a division between us. Our father said, "Because you are brothers!" When we worked in the hayfield, Bo did all the cutting and baling of the hay. The Hells trained only Bo out of all the other kids in the art of cutting hay. Sometimes, my family would talk about the Hells and how they hated us because we were "Niggers" and less than human. Every time the Hells gathered around other whites, they would misuse us badly on purpose. Dad said, "That is to show their white friends that they are superior to us."

Whenever the Hells saw the love and respect between blacks, they tried to create division. Yet, our love for each other was stronger and more powerful than their white supremacy. During that time, I weighed approximately eighty lbs. I was very thin at that time. I recall my nickname "skin" because I was skinny for my age. My brother Bo, on the other hand, was all muscles. He was more valuable than I because he could perform the heavy duties that were expected on the plantation.

Eventually, the family got in touch with our sister Willie B. who lived in Arkansas City. Father made plans for her to come by one day at midnight to steal Bo and me out of Louisiana and off the Hell Plantation. Willie B. planned to pick us up at midnight after everyone on the plantation was asleep. While everyone was tucked away and sleeping, we snuck out of the house and traveled two miles to Don-nell, Louisiana. The next day, we headed north about another mile or two on Highway 17 and hid until midnight. Willie B. left our hiding place momentarily to make sure that it was safe to leave. Finally, she came back, stopped, and called out our names. Bo and I ran out, crying and scared, thinking she had forgotten us. We were so glad to be free and on our way back home to Arkansas. It was only a month or so before Mr. Hell persuaded my father to tell him everything, and dad brought him right to our sister's front door.

She lived down the main road on the Abowitz Plantation. To locate it, one had to walk past two cattle gaps and across the only bridge on the plantation. After passing three shotgun houses on the left, make a left turn, and go to the end of the road to a red four-room house next to the bayou. It was about a mile off the main highway on the Abowitz Plantation, just west of Arkansas City. Dad was with him when he called Willie B., asking her to send the boys out so that they could return with them back to Donnell, Louisiana. But she continued saying the boys were not with her. So, Mr. Hell became angry and said to her, "Tell those nigger boys that if we see them riding or walking in Louisiana, they will die."

By that time, the boss of the Abowitz Plantation had a truckload of both black and Mexican workers with guns and sticks who came to the house and forced the Hells off the plantation. Of course, Mr. Elsie became very angry because he had never been told what to do by people of color.

However, they warned Mr. Elsie never to return. A few months after the Abowitz Plantation workers confronted the Hells, Abowitz sent Willie B. back to Don-nell, Louisiana, to the Hell Plantation in one of his three-quarter-ton trucks with high wooden sides. She stole dad with the rest of the family and brought them back to Arkansas City, and it was a success! Bo and I never went back to Louisiana for many years for fear of our lives. Willie B. tried to tell me to go back to school, but I was too old to go back to the second grade. So, Bo and I started trying to create something, anything, using anything that we could to make music. We would take the wire that held the straws on an old broom and put it on a board and wrap it tight around a nail and make music. We also strung wires between small cans to put them up to our ears and used the cups as a telephone. Gradually, Bo and a white girl named Carolyne Garner got involved. They were caught in the outhouse one night together having sex. Her family reported it downtown to the sheriff department, and they applied pressure on him until the family had to send him away because the whites in town were out to kill him.

Bo was also going with a nice-looking black woman named Robina. She was previously married to Frank Hampton, with whom she had three children. The family pooled their money together and sent Bo to Oakland, California, in 1960, along with Robina, hoping to fix that problem. Bo later got his hands on a small guitar and became a self-taught musician. He had his own entertainment business. He played backup and sang backup for entertainers when they performed shows in the city. He lived with his family in Oakland, California. He had taught himself to play three different instruments before he was killed at the age of forty-three by a young man who demanded money to support a drug habit. I always reminisced how we worked hard and played every day.

One of the memories of Bo and me, along with three other boys, was a lesson we learned walking across the levee from Arkansas City. After swimming in a spot everyone called the blue hole, we learned that it was the most dangerous water body in that area. When the river level had dropped, it created a suck hole and sucked whatever got in the whirlpool under the water, through the bottom of the levee, and deposited it back to the river. It was an underground spring, and as kids, we knew nothing about it, other than that it was not safe. That same day, we swam back and forth across the levee without resting. On my swim back to the other side, I was twenty feet from land. Fatigue hit me, and before I knew it, I was tired and began to sink. Frantically, I called out to Bo, but he was too far away to hear me. Thankfully, someone got his attention that I was in trouble. Once Bo noticed me, he turned around swiftly and jumped back into the water and saved my life. I didn't know anything about God at the time. But moments like this reminded me that God always had a plan for my life.

That was a good day for me, but it turned out to be a bad day for some of the boys. White boys and girls came to the blue hole that day, but some of them refused to get in the water with us. They got in their cars and drove back to town to the sheriff department. The white kids said the black boys were swimming with the white girls. As we left the levee and walked back to the city, the sheriffs met us and arrested us. We did not know why at that time and couldn't figure out why the sheriffs let me go home and kept Bo. He was sent home later by a black sheriff named Mr. Hays. The sheriffs trusted Bo in his hands. The other two black boys served prison time for swimming with white girls.

As I look back, there had to be a God somewhere. Willie B. had always had a good name in Arkansas City. Everyone seemed to respect her. She worked for one of the richest persons in the town named Mr. Gene Kennedy. Black boys were not allowed to flaunt themselves with white girls. Yet, White men were having babies by some of the Black girls, and nothing was done about it. After many years had passed by, I recall that Bo and I were informed that some of the Hells had died. During those days, we were curious to go back and visit members of our family who still lived in Louisiana. When our family returned to the Abowitz Plantation, it wasn't long before another family moved from Dermot, Arkansas. The Daniel family moved on the plantation, and we had all kinds of fun. The Daniels included Jerry, Ernest, Henry, Mary, Lola Mae, and Peaches. Mrs. Mittie was their mother. Henry was the oldest boy, and he was sixteen years old. We worked and had fun every day. None of us went to school. Willie B. told our family that Truedell was pregnant and that she would be coming to stay with her at Abowitz Plantation. At the age of nineteen, Truedell gave birth to a baby boy named Terry in a shotgun house. Willie B. had sent me to get a midwife to help with the delivery, but she had already delivered the baby by the time I came back to the house.

Meanwhile, back in Louisiana, our sister, Geraldine, and Joe moved from Green Bayou Ridge to Del-hi, Louisiana. For years, Truedell and her son Terry traveled back and forth from Arkansas City to Del-hi, Louisiana. Truedell got pregnant again, and this time, she had a cute little girl and named her Barbara Jean. As time passed, Terry was about eleven years of age and out of school for the summer, playing with two of his first cousins in Bayou Mason after a big rain, and he drowned. Some of the kids said the three of them held hands, walked out into the bayou, and drowned under the bridge in Bayou Mason. Terry was the glue that held Truedell and Williams together. After Terry's death, Truedell and William separated. Later, Truedell had another child, a boy, and named him John Earl Johnson by a different man. Even though Truedell and William separated, they lived in the same town for many years as friends. My family had very little education, and some of us had no education. Our reading and writing were limited because we were not allowed to attend school. Education wasn't something that the family talked about. The family had moved back to Arkansas, where everything was better. We lived on the Abowitz Plantation for the next few years, and the family made new adjustments. The Blacks, Whites, and Mexicans lived together.

Willie B. was single for a long time, so she decided to go to Kansas City and stay with Mary Lee for a while to get away. However, she came back to

Arkansas City after a few months. She said that she didn't like the big city. Once she got back home, I moved in with her, leaving my father's house. Meanwhile, Mrs. Geneva decided to leave dad and move far away, taking the girls with her. Dad never found out where she went.

In 1961, once I turned 17 years of age, I ran away from home with some friends to Wichita, Kansas. I did not know how to read. I thought Wichita, Kansas, and Kansas City, Missouri, were the same places. To my surprise, I was miles away from where my sister, Mary Lee, lived. I ran out of money, but my friend's family got me a job at an iron and steel foundry. I ran the grinding machine. It was very hot work, but I learned how to do it. I have the scars on my hands until this day from the grinding machine. And after working a week, I got my check, and they put me on a bus to Kansas City. Unfortunately, I didn't have her address or telephone number, but I was on my way to find her. When I arrived in downtown Kansas City at the bus station, it was so large that I got lost inside it.

The thrill of meeting mary lee

After I arrived in Kansas City, it dawned on me that I didn't have any way of contacting my sister Mary Lee. So, I stayed and slept in the bus station during the nights, and walked around downtown during the day, hoping to see her. Desperately, I tried to get in contact with her. Finally, while walking down 15th Avenue and Truman Road, I passed by a car wash on my way to Woodland Street. Not far from downtown, I decided to walk back to the car wash, hoping to find my sister there. It became a place of interest because people were in and out of the car wash all day long. I thought, "I will surely run into Mary Lee." After hanging around the car wash for days, a worker didn't show up for work, and the manager on duty asked if I wanted a job. Ecstatically, I said yes, and he gave me the job, and I was glad to work because I already had very little money on me then.

The car wash was open seven days a week. I worked every day, and I slept in a small equipment room. Every Sunday, a peculiar man would come to the car wash on his way to church to get his car detailed. One day, he saw me there and asked, "Where do you live?" I said, "Right here in one of the mop rooms." He then asked, "Where is your family?" I told him, "I have a sister named Mary Lee Pounds that lives somewhere in the city, but I don't know where."

He told me he was on his way to church, and if he heard anything about Mary Lee, he would get in touch with me. The next Sunday, we talked about the same thing. This time, after church, he returned to the car wash with good news. He told me he met my sister. Mary Lee was an usher at Morning Star Baptist Church at 2701 Wabash Street. He also told me she lived at 2801 Wabash. It was thirteen blocks away from where I worked. He then asked, "What time you get off?" I told him, "At 5:00 pm." After work, he picked me up and took me to Mary Lee's house, and that was one of the greatest days of my life. Mary Lee had a 14-year-old daughter named Deloris. She took me around Kansas City, Missouri, every chance she got. I lived with them for the next two years. During my time with my niece, Deloris, she taught me many things about the city. She taught me how to read the street signs and how to print my name and how to catch the city bus.

It wasn't my sister's wish to see me in trouble. However, as I walked up and down Prospect Avenue, I got involved with a gang called the Dragon. Mary Lee had warned me to stay away from those types of people. She scolded me to keep a job and try to make something out of myself.

She encouraged me to get honest work. I got a job at Dales Drive Inn restaurant, working and running the dishwasher. There was an older man named Walter who worked the early morning shift. His job was to grind the meat up for burgers. He made small meatballs. He placed them on the grill and mashed them into burgers. Sometimes, I would come in a little early, and he would show me how to prepare the meat for the day shift. Walter told me that he never had a day off. One day, Walter was sick and called in and told the managers that they could call me because he had trained me to prepare the meat for the day's shift. After that incident, they gave him a day off each week and gave me extra hours. So, I worked and saved my money. In 1962, I bought a 1951 Chevrolet, two-door hardtop, dark red with a blacktop. It had a 1951 Corvette six-cylinder engine with

150 horsepower, a three-speed transmission, and a manual floor-mounted stick shift installed on it, which was *very* nice.

My friends and I would go to the racetrack, late in the night, every weekend after work to race our cars. Sometimes we won, and sometimes we lost. Later, I got a promotion from a dishwasher to a cook, which meant I could save more money. So, in 1964, while living with my sister and working at Dales Drive Inn, I saved enough money to make a down payment on a brand-new 1964 Chevrolet. It was black with a red interior. Being young and wild, I took my new car to the racetrack and blew the transmission the second week of ownership. I had it towed to the dealer, and they repaired it free of charge, with no questions asked. I went back to my hometown every year for a week or two. Later, I got a better job with Kansas City, Missouri, the Pollution Control department as a laborer. I had fun working with two older men. They also were laborers. Their job was to clean out the screens so that the wastewater could flow through them easily. They taught me a lot of good and bad stuff. The tall one was an Indian and half black, and the other one was a short black man. The tall one talked about women and sex, and the short one was married. So, he talked about the Bible. But I was too busy trying to do my job and stay out of trouble.

Being involved with a gang, I met a young lady named Faye Mathis. Soon after meeting her, we got married. And for the fun of it, we partied all the time. In 1965, I was drafted into the United States Army, but I could not pass the written examination. I was reclassified (1Y) because I could not read well enough to pass the test. And in 1966, I managed to get out of the gang alive because one could only die out of a gang. In November 1967, I was redrafted. I passed the written examination and enlisted for four years instead of two. If I enlisted for four years, the army would guarantee me two years of stateside for schooling. My reason for accepting their offer was that Faye was pregnant. I wanted to stay close by her until the baby arrived. So, I did my basic training in Fort Campbell, Kentucky, for eight weeks. After graduation, as a Private E-1., I came home only to learn that Faye had miscarried a set of twins.

I stayed home for thirty days before I went to Fort Baker, California, C-Company. I worked as an MSLMN with older men like Staff Sergeant Haley. He was tall, dark, with a beer-belly and had a skinny short wife named Kathrine, but she was a nice woman. Other men taught me how to drink, party, and to be a soldier. Mentally, I couldn't wait to return home to my wife. I went to Oakland, California, to visit my brother Bo and his family. I asked if Faye could live with them until I could move to San Rafael, just a few miles off base. After some time had passed, I met a group of soldiers fresh out of Vietnam. Ulysses was one of the men I met. He knew a young lady who worked just off the base, as a Fair Child conductor.

He paid me to take him out to meet her a few times a week, and that was how I got to see Tenthy for the first time. Ulysses asked if I wanted to meet his girlfriend's friend, and I said no because I was married at the time. And by 1968, I took a leave from the military and went back to Kansas City to pick up my car and my wife, Faye. But she didn't want to leave Kansas City and her friends. Eventually, I convinced her to come to California to live with my brother and his wife until I found an apartment near the base.

After months in our new place, I was on alert status one night and had to stay on the base until the status changed from red to green. I learned that my wife's friend came from Kansas City. He picked her up and another girlfriend and took them to San Francisco along with a fellow soldier's wife. She went to another city with her friend, and there was nothing that I could do about it. After the alert status had changed, I went home. When she returned, I was sitting in the house. I had caught her red-handed, and she did not like it. In 1969, I was promoted from Specialist E-4 to the rank of Specialist E-5. Immediately, I bought my wife a new Chevrolet Camaro burnish brown with a pearl white interior. I had hoped that it would help our relationship, but she said that I was not spending enough time with her. The military sent me before the outstanding soldiers of the quarter board, and I passed it. During the next few months, C-Company was shipping men out to Korea, Vietnam, and Germany. I was sent to Fort Bliss, Texas, for advanced infantry training because our company would soon be deployed. But as soon as Faye and I arrived at Fort Bliss, she caught a bus and went back to Kansas City, Missouri, to her family. I spent the next year training in the desert before I became sick with tonsillitis while packing the equipment for shipping. Three or four weeks before my company was to ship out, I underwent surgery and remained hospitalized, causing me to miss my departure date. Later, I was shipped to Germany as a track commander, ground to air defense, for the Air Force at Hunn Air Force Base. I had been there for approximately six months when the Red Cross contacted me about my wife, Faye. She was sick. Faye had become ill while she was visiting family in Tulsa, Oklahoma. The doctors didn't think that she would make it. So, the Red Cross shipped me back to the United States to Tulsa, Oklahoma. She recovered and returned to Kansas City, where her family lived. I had 15 days of furlough before I needed to return to my assignment in Germany.

I went with my sister, Willie B., to visit our family in Arkansas City. I had a chance to have some fun with my old friends before returning to Germany. A few months later, not knowing that she was in communications with a young man already in Germany, I sent for Faye to join me in Germany. When I brought her over, they connected, and their relationship became stronger. After weeks had passed by, one day, I mistakenly intercepted a love letter from him to her. Meanwhile, she became very ill; so, I carried her to the military doctor. He asked me, "Do you know that you're going to be a father?" I said, "Thanks!" but I knew that the baby was not mine. The love letter was proof. I talked with her, and she told me everything. Thus, she packed her bags, and I took her back to Frankfurt airport to ship her back to the United States. Afterward, I moved back to the base.

At that point in my life, I was already drinking, and I was confused! I started drinking more, getting drunk, hanging out, and missing my military assignments such as the sergeant of the guardsmen. I was disciplined with an article 15 and loss of pay. I also was put in the hospital under quarantine for more than a month for rehabilitation. When I got out, I started hanging out and using drugs with the drug dealers. Gradually, I lost all hope of ever making a career in the military. In the same year, I got injured, taking a friend home that lived off base who needed food and water for his family. I had an accident. I was severely injured. I was carried to the 97th General Hospital in Germany. I had to undergo surgery. They stabilized me. They placed me in a body cast and airlifted me to Andrews Air Force base in America, and from there to Fort Leonard Wood just outside of St. Louis, Missouri.

After Faye heard that I was shipped back to America, she started hounding me for money. She thought that since I was still her husband, she and her man-friend could come to Fort Leonard Wood just to get money from me. A few months past, my brother, Arthur, who lived in Kansas City, heard that I was back in the United States. He started coming out to visit me, and from time to time, he would take me home with him for the weekend. I learned where Faye was living with her man-friend, and my brother Arthur asked if he could kill them for me. I quickly said no. He took me to visit Faye's parents. Seeing us outside, she thought I was spying on her. She got angry and pushed me down in their yard. I couldn't get up because I was in a body cast. She got a baseball bat and beat me with it. My brother stepped out of the car to defend me, but her mother and father blocked him. Her parents did nothing to stop her from beating me.

I started leaving the military base to indulge in drugs and drinking. In my hospital room, I was getting high on uppers, downers, Florida Sunshine, and marijuana. My cousin named Floretta, from Arkansas City, paid me a surprise visit. She took me to Saint Louis, Missouri, to spend the weekend with my sister Willie B.'s husband, Brother R.L. McDaniel. It was a lovely surprise. I didn't leave base anymore, and I stayed on the base for about a year until my discharge date. I served three years, eleven months, and sixteen days. In 1970, I heard, from back home, that my friend, Henry Daniel, who was married to one of my close friends, Katie Robertson, had moved to Boggy Bayou on the Abowitz Plantation. His brother Jerry married his dream girl, Rose Haygood. Many years earlier, their sister Lola had married Katie's father, Mr. Eddie Robertson. She had a daughter before their marriage, and they had a son together.

On November 16, 1971, on crutches, I was discharged from the United States Army at Fort Leonard Wood, Missouri. After a few months, I returned to work at Bendix Corporation. In 1975, Henry and Katie Daniel moved to the Big House so that he could oversee the Abowitz Plantation for the owner, Mr. Maurice Abowitz. In the late nineties, Henry was honored by the owner, and he became the first black man to be recognized because he was the first black man to be over the plantation and to have a road named after him. He died in 2001. Before his demise, he had worked for the Abowitz since he was sixteen years of age. Afterward, Mr. Abowitz decided to sell the land to Bill Fred. On July 4, 2011, in honor of Henry Daniel, they named the road traveling through the plantation "Henry Daniel Lane."

My New Life With Jesus

For years, I was not a Christian. I lived a lifestyle of drugs, women, smoking cigarettes, using profanities, and drinking alcohol almost excessively. While working at Bendix, as a janitor, I had many "so-called-friends," but I considered Rich and Sam as my best friends. We did everything together. Sam and I worked together at Bendix and had other different jobs in different areas. He tried everything that he knew to introduce Tenthy to me, but I refused his offers. When I was stationed in California, God had already shown Tenthy to me. I didn't respect God. From my perspective, God was a white man trying to enslave the mind and body of black people. Clearly, my view was warped by my past experiences on the Hell Plantation. I had promised myself that when I became a freeman, I would be my own god.

While in California, I was transferred to Fort Bliss in El Paseo, Texas, for advanced cadre training. After training at Maguire Airbase in the desert for a year, my company was readily deployed. I recall Tenthy saying that after a year, she would move from California to Brownsville, Tennessee, to be with her parents. However, Tenthy moved to Kansas City, Missouri, to live with her brother, Alonzo Beard, and later came to work at the Bendix Corporation as a trainee in the red badge area. Sam had already met her and the other trainees. So, he offered to buy me lunch so that he could introduce the two of us. One Friday, when I met her, I could not believe that she was not an angel. She was so pretty. I could not see myself with her. We engaged in friendly conversations. Since I didn't have a car, I was not able to take her on a date. After she completed her training, we continued talking during our lunch breaks at work. One day, while we talked, she said that she could not date me, and I asked her, "Why not?" Tenthy said, "Because you are a devil and not a Christian." At the time, she didn't want to go through the headaches of dating a man that did not share her religious convictions. One Sunday, I decided to check her out. So, I followed her to church without her knowing it. I sat in the parking lot just to see what was going on and why she was so interested in church.

When the church service was over, Pastor Jerry Walker walked outside with Tenthy. I was so embarrassed. I slid down in my seat so that they could not see me. I was already being hounded by this preacher named Curry and his deacon, Frank K. Johnson. I could not make one step without hearing them trying to tell me about this white man called Jesus Christ. They tried to tell me that He was God's Son, and I didn't want to hear it. One day, I heard Tenthy was sick. Her mother had come from Tennessee to stay with her until she recovered. One day, I went to see her after work and to meet her mother, Mrs. Hellen. It was unusual for me to feel close to someone that soon. She was the type of lady that I would have wanted for a mother. Unfortunately, I only had small memories of my mother. After Tenthy had recovered, she started making plans to go to Tennessee for a family reunion. She asked if I would ride to Tennessee with her. Of course, I said yes, not knowing what a reunion was. I had a chance to meet her father and her family. They were nice people.

Her father invited me to sit with him outside on large white stones in his yard. He asked questions about my life. He helped me understand why man was created and what his purpose in life should be. I also met her brother, Henry; he and I got along right away. Henry and I would go to the tractor shed to drink beer and smoke. No one else knew what we were doing. One Sunday, I went to church with the family. For the first time in my life, I saw a cloud within the church, and when it got to me, I got high. After church, I told Henry about the high that I experienced inside the church, and it was free. It was better than any high that I had ever had. That experience never left me.

One month later, back in Kansas City, I decided to work one Saturday. Hence, I went to work late on purpose, hoping to be alone. Deacon Frank Johnson came to work late that morning also, and he was on the job working with me.

Around 11:00 am that morning, Deacon Frank began to sing "Amazing Grace," and I didn't know the song. I didn't like it. Yet, he kept singing it repeatedly. While listening to him singing his song, my spirit began to listen to the lyrics of the song. I began to pay attention to what the song was saying. For the first time, I heard the words with understanding. Consumed in the moment, the Holy Spirit came into my heart, and I had an out of body experience. God saved me that Saturday, just before lunch, in November 1972. And after a few months, Tenthy started talking to me again, mostly about Jesus. God sent her because I needed spiritual advice. She was attending Saint Jude. So, I attended Saint Jude with her under the leadership of Pastor Jerry Walker.

The Lord knew that I desired a companion, and in His time, He gave me the wife of His choice. God brought Tenthy all the way from California to Brownsville, Tennessee, to Kansas City, Missouri, and then to the Bendix Corporation. Look at God! I had finished my tour in the military, and my last years were in Fort Leonard Wood, Missouri, where I was discharged on November 17, 1971. After a few months, I was well enough to work. I didn't know God at that time, but He always had plans for me. It was God's plan for Walter to buy my lunch so that I could meet and talk with Tenthy in the red badge lunching area. The more we talked, the more she looked like an angel. While we talked, she would grin and say, "You are a devil." Smiling, I would say, "Yes, I am. But I'm a good devil." She would say, "No way!" I was aware of good and evil, but I didn't understand why it was legal for whites to abuse blacks. Why were blacks expected to be submissive, and when we resisted, it cost us pain? It had been about nine months since I was saved, and we dated for about seven months before we got married.

On June 29, 1973, Rev. Dr. I. H. Henderson married us. Saint Steven Missionary Baptist Church had a very large congregation. The two of us later joined Emmanuel Baptist Church, 920 Olive Street, under the leadership of Dr. W. H. White, where we trained in the mission of the church. In 1976, Dr. White trained me to serve as a deacon of the church. Tenthy and I became co-founders of the Jail Prison Outreach Deliverance Ministries. We did street ministry and went all over the state of Missouri. We also participated in weekly radio broadcastings, and we traveled weekly to different prisons. While attending Penn Valley Community College, I joined a group of young missionaries, and we did mission work during our lunch breaks. We had fun serving the Lord.

Tenthy and I lived at 1729 Woodland Avenue, and we evangelized the local area. I was able to do funerals with the former Bruce Watkin Funeral Home and the Jones Funeral Home. From 1976 to 1984, we did ministry all over Missouri and Kansas. My father Zeb called me in May 1984 and gave me the best news ever. He told me that he had accepted Jesus Christ as his Lord and Savior and asked if I could come home on his birthday, June 27th, and speak at his church. I was so excited that my father had become a Christian. But sad news came to our house on June 2nd. My sister, Willie B., called and informed me that Dad had died that night after he left her house. He lived next door. She said that after turning on the light in his bedroom, she went back into her house. When he didn't show up for breakfast the next morning, she went over to his house and found him beside his bed on his knees, dead. She was shocked, but she wanted me to come home. I was asked to do the eulogy. However, my wife Tenthy had just undergone surgery and could not go with me.

Since Tenthy was not able to travel, I asked a good friend, Reverend Donald Morrison, to ride with me. The service was held at Zion Hill Missionary Baptist Church in Arkansas City, Arkansas. My father Zeb was laid to rest at Sunny Side graveyard, where our mother and other family members were buried.

While our daughter, Cynthia, attended Oral Roberts University for two years, Tenthy and I lived in Kansas City, Missouri. On June 17, 1984, we heard a call from God to start a new mission in Tennessee. However, Cynthia wanted to stay in Kansas City to attend school. While we were still in Kansas City, I had communicated with Fort Pillow Penitentiary, in Tennessee, about a job. When they considered my request and reviewed my credentials, I was hired over the phone and asked when I could report for work. My son traveled with me so that I could report for work on time. He and I returned to Kansas City in August to finish moving my wife to Tennessee. Shortly after she joined us, we joined her family church, St. Luke Missionary Baptist, under the leadership of Rev. Glenn Strickland.

We lived with her father and mother in Haywood County, on their family farm. I had applied for employment with the United States Postal Service, and in May of 1985, I received a call from the U.S. Post Office, informing me that I had been hired. In September, my wife's parents' home burned to the ground a few days before the family reunion. We lost everything that we had brought from Kansas City. Tenthy and I had to find a place to stay. Her sister, Verner Dean Thompson, invited us to stay in her home. Later, we moved from Haywood County to Lauderdale County in Ripley, Tennessee. We worked with Pastor Dr. Willie Lewis Reid of Holly Grove, and with the surrounding churches. Pastor Dr. W. L. Reid asked me to teach his church street ministry, and for the next eight weeks, we held night classes, then we evangelized East End and Gay Streets.

I preached throughout the five-county area as a member of Saint Luke Missionary Baptist Church. In 1984, I joined the Mississippi Valley District Association, which was a member of the Tennessee Baptist Missionary and Education Convention. In 1989, God spoke to Deacon Melvin Brook, a member of St. Paul Missionary Baptist Church of Kenton, Tennessee. He called and asked me to preach one night during their five-night revival. It was held on Wednesday in June 1989, and after the five nights of service and five preachers, I was asked to preach in August. And for the next five months, each one of the revival preachers was to preach for a month. After I had preached in August, the next preacher was called to another church. By November, the congregation of St. Paul Missionary Baptist Church decided to install me as their pastor in 1989.

In late 1989, I joined the Volunteer Chaplin Association with the Lauderdale Baptist Hospital, where I am presently serving. That same year, I enrolled in the R.G. Lee Center, an extension of Union University, for a part-time program, one class per semester. In 2001, I was appointed Dean of the Congress of Christian Education in the Mississippi Valley District Association. And In 2003, I graduated with the largest graduating class at Union University and received a Diploma in Ministry. Having to travel back and forth to McGehee, Arkansas, to visit my sister, Willie B., in the nursing home, I dropped out of school for several years. She was hospitalized many times, and later, she was transferred to Pine Bluff Arkansas Hospital, where they implanted a pacemaker. Months later, she underwent triple bypass heart surgery. Tenthy and I traveled to Pine Bluff sometimes every week to be with her for two or three days during her hospital stays. She later went to Monticello, Arkansas, for rehab. She finished her rehab, and she was finally allowed to return to Arkansas City to live in the new home that she built. After eight or nine months, her home was badly burned. Unfortunately, she was placed in and out of the nursing homes in McGehee, Arkansas.

Tenthy and I traveled from Ripley, Tennessee, to Pine Bluff, Arkansas, each week to be with Willie B. until she was able to travel. She would eventually live near us in a nursing home in Ripley, Tennessee. Now, we could visit her daily. On the weekends, we would bring her home to fellowship with the Beards and Pounds family dinners. One day, Tenthy was out of town, and I wanted to take Willie B. out, so I bought her a beautiful pink dress for that special day. That day, the two of us had a "ball" and just shopped around. On our way back, we stopped by the Olympics' Steak House for dinner and had an awesome time together. She also joined St. Paul Baptist Church, where I pastored. We took her best-dress-church clothes to the nursing home every Sunday morning. They would dress her for us, and all we had to do was help her to the car and off to Church we would go. She was always excited to tell Tenthy and me that she was very proud of us and what we always did for her.

She thoroughly enjoyed watching me preach and sing in the male chorus. God blessed me to travel to the Philippines Islands for the first time with Dr. Charles Pratts in 2007. The first time I went overseas, Willie B. told me she prayed for me until I was back home and in her room. In 2011, I teamed up with Minister Detra Wade and traveled to Nigeria in West Africa to preach in Mega Fest. We traveled the country of Nigeria preaching in the streets, ministering medical aid, praying for deliverance, casting out demons, feeding the hungry, and giving out clothes to the needy. I always brought back gifts for Willie B. and my wife. Tenthy and I took Willie B. to the Pounds and Hedgeman's family reunion in Del-hi, Louisiana, and visited several cities in Tennessee. In June 2014, she really wanted to go with Tenthy and me to Del-hi, Louisiana, to the family reunion so she could see her new grandbabies. But her doctor said no. I promised her that I would take pictures and videos of her grandkids. When I arrived back at the nursing home, I showed her the pictures and videos. Viewing how her grandbabies grew over time, Willie B. could not contain her swollen emotions. She just cried for joy. We didn't know that would be her last time visiting the family reunion or looking at the pictures. That same year, she encouraged me to stay enrolled at Union University. Willie B said, "Please graduate! Make yourself and the family proud!"

On October 4, 2014, Willie B., my sister—my second mother for most of my life—and the person who named me, passed the baton of being the oldest to me. She went home to be with Jesus. That was a sad and lonely day in my life, and my wife Tenthy was right by my side. Thank God for her spiritual, physical, and emotional support. It was in 2014 that the Holy Spirit led me with the support of my sister-in-law, Dr. Hetty Jones, my niece, Carolyne, and my eldest granddaughter, Merissa, to continue my education. Merissa had earned her bachelor's degree from Roads College and a master's degree from Union University in education. She wanted us to have a degree from the same University so that we would have a bond of being Grandfather and Granddaughter, frat brother and sister. She always encouraged me to do my best in my educational endeavors. I was motivated to continue my studies, and I was blessed to graduate on December 17, 2016, with a BSOL Degree in Organizational Leadership Church Consecrations from Union University.

The Union University president asked me if I had any plans to further my education, and I said yes. I was offered an opportunity to pursue my master's degree. Immediately, I went back to register for the courses of my major. I had less than thirty days to notify the department and choose a major before classes started. I chose Theology and Mission.

I pastored in Kenton, Tennessee, next door to First Baptist Church, where Reverend Dr. Charles Pratt, a good friend of mine, served as Pastor. He encouraged me to continue going on missionary trips to the Republic of Philippines islands with him and the Cross Partners Ministries. Fellowshipping with Cross Partners Ministries has changed my whole life. I've served faithfully on missionary trips to the islands since 2007. On September 8, 2019, my wife and I celebrated my thirtieth Pastoral Anniversary at St. Paul Missionary Baptist Church, where I'm the senior pastor.

The Family Photo Gallery

Cube Coger   Mammie Jones Coger

Mother Bessie Mae
Sister Bestell

My Father Zeb & Mother
Bessie Mae
Sister Bestell

Willie D. (12 Month)

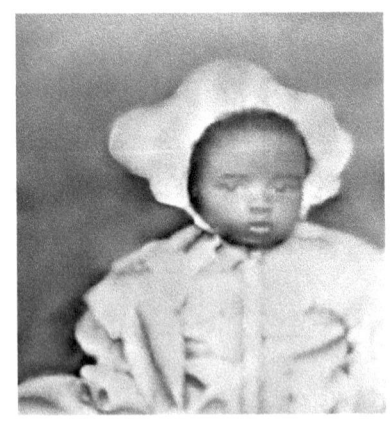

Willie Lee (13 Months)

Truedell Louis

Bud Watson

Ann Uncle Edmond, My Father Zeb,
Sister Mary Lee

Left to Right: Arthur II, Jessie,
Arthur A. I., Andrea Pounds

Willie Lee & Deloris (Niece)

Back Row: Left to Right: Willie B, Geraldine
Mary Lee, Aunt Truedell, Sister Truedell
Second Row: Jessie, Bestell
Kneeling Down: L-R: Arthur, Willie Lee

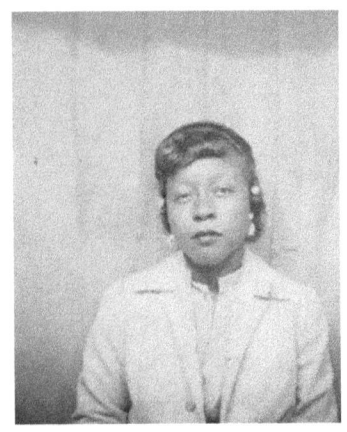
Geraldine Hedgeman

Mammie Jones & Son Forest

Ezell & Willie D.

Nephew Adolph & Sister Geraldine

TWO AND ONE-HALF YEARS IN HELL ON EARTH

Grandfather Cubie

Mother's Sister Truedell

Sister Mary Lee

Brother Zeb, Junior

REVEREND WILLIE L. POUNDS

Kneeling: Arthur, Willie Lee

Back Row: Bestell, Mary Lee
Middle Row: Lora, Jessie & Geraldine
Front Row: Unknown

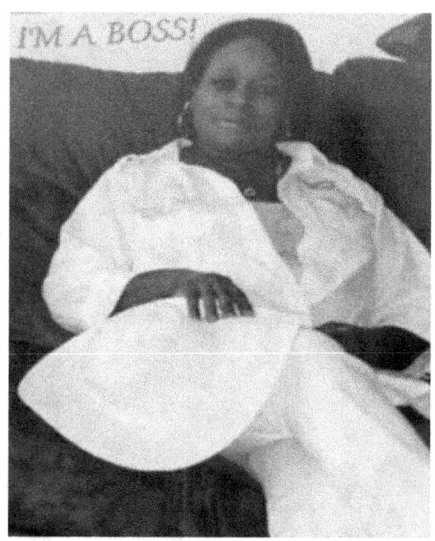

Barbara (Niece)

Back Row: Barbara, Willie Lee, Ezell
Willie D, Mary Lee & Husband Wendell, Willie B
Front Row: Adeline & Husband Roy

REVEREND WILLIE L. POUNDS

Willie Lee Pounds

TWO AND ONE-HALF YEARS IN HELL ON EARTH

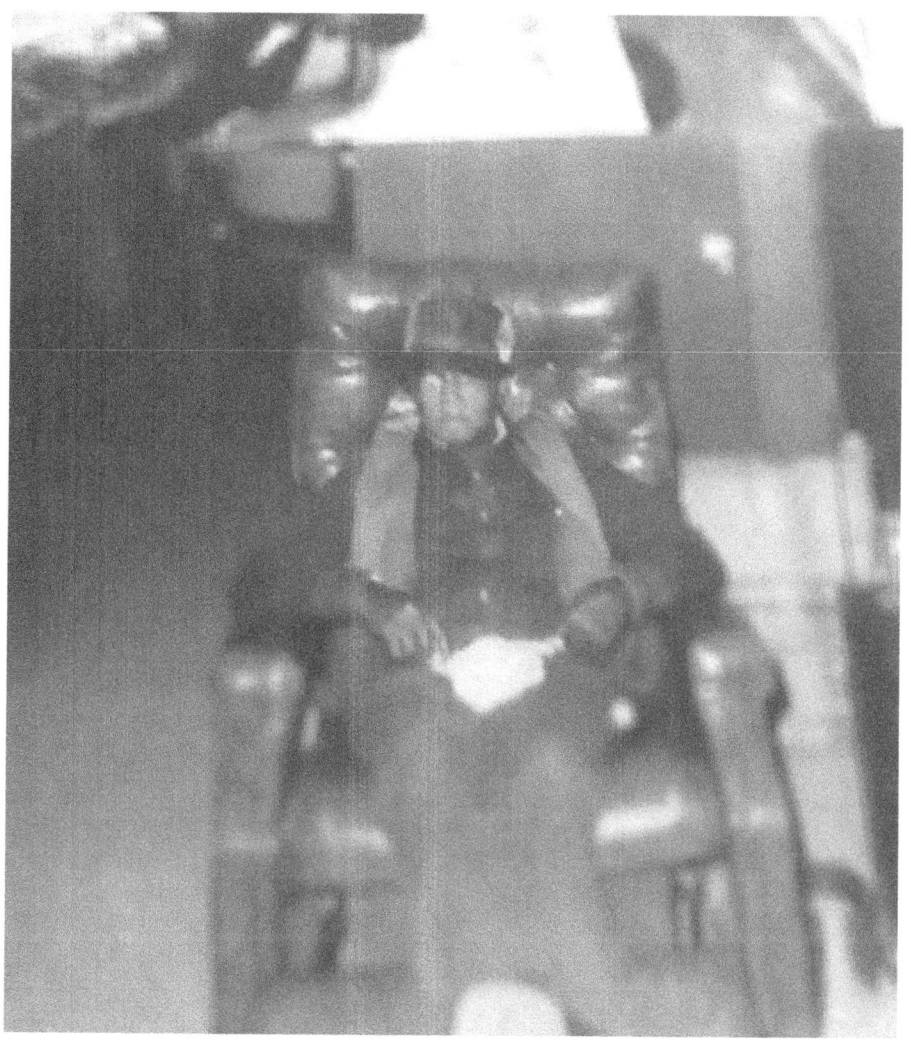

My Father
Zeb Pounds

www.ingramcontent.com/pod-product-compliance
Lightning Source LLC
Chambersburg PA
CBHW071031080526
44587CB00015B/2576